Joan of Arc

A Joan of Arc Biography

Anna Revell

Table of Contents

Introduction

France was at a point of crisis. It was in some ways on the edges of ruin, barely holding onto itself under the attacks of a foreign power, over a decades' long war that had even turned Frenchman against Frenchman. The country's territories were splintered among different loyalties. The French heir to the throne of a long-mad, dead king has been disinherited and pushed to the south, while England's infant king and his champions held a hold on the north and were starting a stronger push southward.

It was the year 1429 and almost a century into the Hundred Years' War, the English had the upper hand. They had a string of key victories, sometimes against unfathomable odds, and had the territory to show for it – including Paris. They also had an alliance with a powerful faction of Frenchmen, the Burgundians, and had inked an advantageous treaty that was designed to secure the French throne for England. The heir of King Charles VI of France, the Dauphin Charles of Valois, insisted the throne was rightfully his but practically speaking, he was not unlike "The King of Bourges," as he was sometimes mockingly called after the court he kept in the city. He couldn't even be crowned according to hundreds of years of French tradition, which was to be anointed with holy oil at the Cathedral of Reims in territories outside his influence.

The Dauphin, it has been said, was tiring of war. He could not get his countrymen together. His army was demoralized after suffering many losses. The strategic city of Orléans had been under siege for months. The French garrison inside it was being starved out by a chain of English fortresses surrounding it on three sides, and the prospects of sending successful reinforcements to break the siege seemed poor. The fall of Orléans, which seemed at hand, would give the English forces a key position to strike against his hold on the south.

But an unlikely heroine came from nowhere to change the tide. A teenaged girl - passionate, insistent, relentless and so certain of her God-given calling - came to call upon him at his fortress in Chinon. She wanted men at arms. She wanted to serve her God through her dauphin. In return she offered him victory. Whether by design or by her sheer existence, she also offered her countrymen courage and hope.

From the outset it seemed she had little to offer other than her word. But soon words became backed up by proof – prophecies coming true, capabilities that would not have been accessible to a simple "Maid" from Domrémy, an unexpected eloquence in defense of her beliefs... And then proof grew into legend. And legend rallied her countrymen and struck fear in their foes. And that refreshed rally eventually helped lead her country into victory, even though she herself would not be alive to see it.

For all too soon it all came to an end for this "Maid." She barely had two years in public life before she was captured, ransomed to her enemies, interrogated, charged, tried and martyred. Her stunning brilliance was cut short by the flames of an execution pyre. It was said that her body was burned three times and her ashes scattered. She was only 19 years old.

Her ascent was as quick as her fall. She was the farming tenant's daughter who somehow ended up standing beside the King she helped crown, only to be eventually given up by her own countrymen. She was uneducated but held her own against learned men from two countries, eloquent and sure of her divine call. She lived and acted in the certainty she was a messenger from God, but she was burned at the stake for heresy. Centuries later, she would be canonized as a saint. She continues to be a lightning rod of inspiration to her country, to women, and to millions all over the world who share her faith.

This was Joan of Arc:

The Maid – "*La Pucelle*" – who, compelled by the voices of saints, set out on a mission from God to free her country and crown its dauphin as King. But first, she had to overcome her background and convince her people to listen and take a chance on a possibly mad, uneducated, inexperienced peasant girl from the farms of Domrémy.

The War Hero, whose feats in breaking the English siege at the strategic city of Orléans, came at a crucial point of the Hundred Years' War. Territories have been lost by France and her army was demoralized after a string of major defeats. The dauphin was disinherited and rapidly tiring of war, and the English was knocking on the doors of the French strongholds, making their way south – only to be rebuffed by *La Pucelle* and her army.

The Heretic, betrayed by her own countrymen, sold to her enemies, tried in a foreign-held land and judged false, she had fallen from the impossible heights of her unlikely victories, experienced defeats, outlived her political usefulness, and her faith brutally challenged. She was eventually executed, burning in anguish at the stake, her mouth uttering calls to Jesus until she died. At only 19 years old, the "Maid of Orléans" paid the ultimate price for playing the role of God's angelic messenger in the cruel medieval games of kings and princes.

The Icon, eventually recognized for the authenticity of her message, the exceptional miracle of her achievements and her impact on the faithful, she was declared a saint hundreds of years after her brutal execution. She has since transcended the original purpose of her life. Beyond France, she is a beloved figure to Catholics, women, and various sectors of society. Her contributions continue to be studied and debated. Her legend shared, parsed, dissected. Her mystery continues to draw in wonder and awe. Her powerful image, is almost always in some use for a variety of causes.

This is almost a miracle in itself; her most memorable feats spanned barely two years, yet she remains relevant to countless people, thousands of years after her short, impactful life.

The Maid

Jehanne d'Arc was born around 1412 in the village of Domrémy, France, the daughter of tenant farmers, Jacques d'Arc and his wife, Isabelle Romée. Her exact birthdate is unknown, but what is widely accepted stems from a 1429 letter by a certain Perceval de Boullainvillers which mentions her birth during the date of Epiphany (celebrated by Christians on January 6th) of 1412.

As the question of her birthday suggests, for so famous a figure with a highly documented later life, there are a lot of gaps in our basic knowledge of Joan. Even her name carries complexities. She is widely known as the Anglicized "Joan of Arc" following her father Jacques' surname. But that does not necessarily mean the family came from "Arc," and Jacques may have also been known as "Jacob d'Arc," "Jaqe d'Arc," "Jacques Tarc" or even "Darc"). Joan might have even been known as "Jehanne Romée," for in her hometown, girls took their mother's name. Not that "Romée" as a surname was also straightforward in terms of indicating parentage. It was usually used to refer to someone who had gone on pilgrimage either to Rome or some other religious destination. In short - medieval France was not exactly tied by hard and fast rules on surnames.

Joan's father, Jacques carried some cachet as a relatively prosperous farmer in their small village community. The family was far from wealthy though, and Joan had a simple, domestic life. She was not educated in reading and writing, but her devout mother turned her toward the teachings of the Catholic Church. Joan was a strong-willed but pious girl who cared for their animals, gathered the harvest and was also described as a good spinner and seamstress.

At around the age of 13, she began to experience visions and hear voices from Catholic figures. During her later trial, she shared that the first time she heard voices, she was in her family's garden and saw a bright light and sounds coming *"from the direction of the church."* Ringing church bells sometimes heralded the voices. Experiences like these would happen to her again and again for the rest of her short life. She described encounters with the warrior-saint, St. Michael the Archangel, and the defiant virgin martyrs, St. Catherine of Alexandra and St. Margaret of Antioch.

Their message to the simple peasant girl?

She was tasked with the divine mission of ridding France of the English presence, and crowning the French dauphin, Charles VII, its rightful King.

The Hundred Years' War

Joan lived in a tumultuous time for her country. When she was born, France was already long-embroiled in a conflict with England in what would be called "The Hundred Years' War," from 1337 to 1453. The main issue had been legitimate succession of the French throne after Charles IV of France died in 1328 without a son. He was succeeded by his first cousin and the former Count of Valois, King Philip VI. Edward III of England, however, also had a claim that some corners contested was more valid; he was the late Charles IV's closest male relation, because his mother was Charles IV's sister. Furthermore, in Medieval Europe, kings were able to inherit titles beyond their own kingdoms. Thus, at the time of Charles IV's passing, Edward III of England, holding his inherited titles of Count of Ponthieu and Duke of Guyenne (which was in Aquitaine on French soil), was in a sense also his vassal.

Philip VI succeeded his cousin Charles IV by determination of a French assembly, and this for a time seemed to be acceptable to Edward III. However, Philip VI's confiscation of the duchy of Guyenne from England in 1337 was considered provocation enough to spark an escalation of the tensions. Edward III pursued his claim on the French throne and kicked off the war with an army dispatched to Flanders, thus beginning a conflict that would drag on for over a century... Not that the two countries really harbored much love for each other at the time. The events of 1337 was just one iteration of a larger, intermittent conflict between the two countries that some historians trace all the way back to the Norman Conquest of 1066, and that some would posit as not really ending all the way until the *Entente Cordiale* of 1904. Whether or not one subscribes to this belief, what is important to note is that the weight of heated history is heavy between France and England, such that iconic French politician Charles de Gaulle could go so far as to say – as recently as 1962 – that the country's *"greatest hereditary enemy"* was them, even more than Germany.

The Hundred Years' War was brutal on many levels of French and English life, and one could see characteristics of "total war" in how some of it was conducted. The concept of "total war" wouldn't be articulated and dissected until more modern times (beginning with military strategist Carl von Cluasewitz's work in the 19th century), but what had happened in France in the 14th century seemed to fit the characteristics of an almost no-holds-barred approach toward getting a decisive victory. Large populations of the tax-paying French peasantry, for example, were hard hit by raids called "*Chevauchée*" even if they were non-combatants; as vital sources of revenue that eventually funded military pursuits, they were considered by the likes of England's "The Black Prince" Edward, for example, to be logical targets. Aside from economic reasons, they were also targeted to demoralize and discredit their rulers, and to give the raiding soldiers a financial incentive. In Edward's "*grande chevauchée*" in the 1350s, for example, estimates at the time pegged unprecedented devastation of 500 settlements and 18,000 square kilometers of French territory. The conflict between the two countries, therefore, was deep-seated, long-running and not only limited to the military fields or certain sectors of society, but was palpable in the daily lives of many people.

In Joan of Arc's home village of Domrémy, for example, there were several run-ins with soldiers involved in the Hundred Years' War. The village church was burned at one point, and Joan had to herd the family livestock away from violence on a couple of occasions.

Among the most important battles of the early stages of the Hundred Years' War were the Battle of Crecy in northern France in 1346, which ended in a disastrous defeat for the French in spite of their larger numbers; the Battle of Poitiers in 1356, in which Edward III of England's son, Edward the Black Prince, had actually succeeded in capturing the French king, John II (son of Philip VI, who perished in 1350); and the Battle of Agincourt of 1415, an English victory immortalized by William Shakespeare in his play, *Henry V* (which contains one of the most rousing lines of literature of all time, *"We few, we happy few, we band of brothers; For he to-day that sheds his blood with me, Shall be my brother…"*).

In short, the war dragged on for so long that its initial principal characters would die long before it was even close to ending, and the countries involved in it ended up having to face an international war along with a myriad of their own internal struggles.

In the three battles abovementioned, for example, the first was a victory in Edward III of England's time, but the second was a victory over a France now under his original enemy's son, John II. John II died while in captivity and *his* son, Charles V of France, would be the one to continue the war. Charles V's own son Charles VI, however, would have mental issues which ushered in a whole other set of succession problems within France. This eventually led to a civil war between the Armagnacs and

Burgundians. That internal conflict was one of the reasons why King Henry V of England, taking advantage of the French discord, reignited the English claim to the French throne. Not that the English monarchy did not have major upheavals of its own along the length of the Hundred Years' War. Henry V, after all, was the product of his father, Henry IV's unseating of Edward III's successor, Richard II.

This then, was the world that a simple French peasant girl named Joan, entered. There was a protracted war between the French and the English. It was a war that was "national" in its wide-ranging effects on a large bulk of the populace. There was conflict without, but also conflict within in a France fractured by internal intrigue. The English King Henry V even had Frenchmen on his side – he had forged an alliance with the Burgundians under Philip the Good, the Duke of Burgundy. Henry V's military successes, coupled with the Armagnac assassination of Philip the Good's father, John, reportedly motivated the Burgundians to side with the English.

The alliance between the English king and French Burgundians gave rise to the Treaty of Troyes in 1420. Under the treaty, Henry V would become the mad French King Charles VI's heir, disinheriting his dauphin, Charles of Valois (later, Charles VII). Henry V, who would wed Charles VI's daughter, Catherine, was to be Charles VI's regent while he was alive and after his death, Henry V would claim the French throne. He would therefore become he King of the "double monarchies" of England and France.

It should be noted that the abovementioned major battles of the Hundred Years' War were victories for England, often against dramatic odds. The 1420 treaty also gave them a firm grip on their French interests. Indeed at many points, the ultimate victors of the Hundred Years' War, the French, seemed to find itself on the losing end.

That would change after a teenage peasant girl, claiming to hear the voices of saints giving her a divine mission, entered the picture.

War Hero

What can a seemingly inconsequential little French girl from the country - barely in her adulthood, uneducated, possibly addled and female at a time when a woman's roles were desperately limited – possibly contribute in a long war conducted by a rotating gallery of mighty princes and kings? Why should anyone expect anything from Jehanne d'Arc of Domrémy, when two world powers and nearly a century of military and diplomatic expertise had already been brought to bear by powerful men in a conflict that still seemingly had no decisive end?

Such was the charisma, and/or perhaps her God-given knowledge and authority (if one subscribed to such beliefs), that she was able overcome her background and assert her way first into the court of the Dauphin Charles, then onto the battlefields armed with considerable assets, and eventually into unforgettable, rousing victory at the city of Orléans.

The Road to Orléans

Joan of Arc had a tremendous number of obstacles before she could even head to the city that would make her a legend and later, a national icon and saint. Among these obstacles were the expectations set upon her as a woman of her time. When she was 16 years old, her family reportedly made an attempt to secure for Joan an arranged marriage. But she had taken a vow of chastity in relation to her divine mission, which had at that point been a presence in her heart and mind for years. Joan reportedly even had to appear at a local court to convince authorities to spare her from the match. Virginity was prized at the time in their society, perhaps even more than marriage. She had actually taken to referring to herself as Jehanne la Pucelle – "Joan the Maid," with the "maid" as a signifier of chastity. Either way, thus freed from a marriage she did not want, she was able to pursue her appointed work.

Guiding Voices. The divine mission that moved her was one that would be gradually revealed to her and that she would be groomed and counseled for by three saintly voices. These were the voices of St. Michael the Archangel; Saint Catherine of Alexandria; and Saint Margaret of Antioch. Less prominently, there had also been mention of her experiences with Saint

Gabriel. It is important to understand the background of her three main saintly influences, given their significance to the trajectory of Joan of Arc's life.

Saint Michael was the first among them to connect with Joan, when she was around 13 years old. She had to see him many times before realizing who he was. Archangel Michael is the patron saint of law enforcement and soldiers. He is often depicted in wings and armor, with a weapon drawn in a mighty stance over a serpent. The military connection is apparent in Joan's life, but Saint Michael was also patron to France's royal house at the time, as well as being a known champion of women due to his protection of Mother Mary – which are all relevant to Joan of Arc's specific situation.

The Saints Catherine of Alexandria and Margaret of Antioch (who is also known as Marina), served as protectors and counselors of Joan too, and their histories ended up having remarkable similarities. Saint Margaret, daughter of a pagan priest, converted to Christianity and consecrated herself to God. Thus, she rejected the marriage proposal of a prefect who thereafter had her sent to prison, had her tortured, and subject to a public trial. She was executed by beheading. Saint Catherine, a noblewoman from Alexandria, converted to Christianity too and openly challenged her Emperor's persecution of the faith. She was offered an advantageous marriage to renounce her Christianity, but again like Saint Margaret, she had also taken a vow of chastity. She was sent to prison and her faith repeatedly challenged, but she was able to stand up for her beliefs so gracefully and eloquently that conversions followed in her wake. Saint Catherine was eventually tortured and beheaded. Like these two saints, Joan of Arc was a virgin martyr who had to stand up to authority for her beliefs. At several important points of her life, her faith would be repeatedly challenged too, only for her to conduct herself with contagious passion and intelligence. She was almost like another Saint Catherine and indeed, many people of her time had described her as such.

It was Saint Michael who told Joan she would also be counseled by the Saints Catherine and Margaret. Over the next four years of her life, these gentle saints steered her into preparations for a mission she did not immediately grasp until she turned 17.

Before that time, her instructions were to be a good child of God and a virgin with a holy life lived according to His will. Around the time she turned 17, Saint Michael became a more frequent presence, and he eventually revealed to Joan her purpose in the freeing of her country. She initially doubted her capabilities as a *"poor girl who knew nothing of riding and warfare,"* but eventually understood that if God was commanding her to go, then go she must. With the help of these voices whom she considered her guardians, she had comfort, courage and direction – sometimes even forewarnings of danger – that aided her in her unprecedented campaign.

In 1428, her village in Domrémy was attacked by English and Burgundian forces, necessitating her family to flee until it was safe again. Other than that, she did not really leave home much and indeed, the next (and last) time that she left it, she was in pursuit of her destiny. She needed to gain an an audience with the man she felt duty-bound to crown as the King of France. Geography and her status, however, worked in concert to prevent her from seeing the Dauphin.

Charles held France south of the Loire River; Domrémy was in the east. Though much of Joan's locale was still loyal to Charles, surrounding territories were not necessarily so, with some areas holding loyalty with the English-allied Duchy of Burgundy. It was not going to be an easy journey, even if she could get anyone to believe her and bring her to where Charles held a stronghold in Chinon.

She began her journey at the behest of the voice of Saint Michael. She set off from Domrémy toward the village of Burey-le-Petit, where a relative, Durand Lassois resided. She spoke to him of her mission over a stay of several days and he, taken by her determination, brought her to Vaucouleurs, a place held by loyalists to the dauphin, Charles. There, she sought out a local official named Sir Robert de Baudricourt. She told him of her intent to see Charles in Chinon to convince the dauphin of her mission, and that she needed Sir Robert's men and resources to get there. Accounts of his response range from laughing at her to sending her away to advising that what the girl needed as *a good slapping*" and to be sent back to her father. Either way, he gave her a series of rejections. But Joan was relentless, and she had an ace up her sleeve – a prophecy. She told Sir Robert of a specific French military defeat (later to be known as The Battle of Herring), which would only later be reported by a messenger. It also helped that she was winning over the villagers. Sir Robert de Baudricourt was soon on board with Joan's desire to see the dauphin, and how – he is said to have outfitted her with a sword, a horse and an entourage comprising of a knight, squire and four men. For security reasons, Joan had to travel from Vaucouleurs with cropped hair and dressed like a man.

They traveled an uneventful 150 leagues in 11 days over unsecured territory, and eventually arrived in Chinon, where Joan wrote Charles to request an audience. The dauphin needed some convincing. He consulted with his counselors and men of the church to determine whether or not he should receive her which, as we know from our history, he eventually did… but not without one more test. Charles famously switched clothes with a substitute and mixed in with the sizeable crowd of courtiers, who were curious to see the young girl claiming to be sent by God. Joan did not disappoint. She famously spotted him right away thanks to the voices that had always guided her. She told him of her mission to free France from the English, which included his anointing as the King of France.

The Anointing of a French King

The Dauphin, Charles, was in many ways, already a king when Joan of Arc sought him out in Chinon in 1429. When his father Charles VI died in 1422, by some theorists, he was already the King even without an official coronation. This sensibility may be summarized by the famous words, *"The King is dead. Long live the King!"* Even prior to his ill father's death, he had already been working as regent. Some, however, believe that a coronation confers spiritual legitimacy upon the sovereign. According to this belief, crowning recognizes the supreme authority of God, and that an anointing ceremony is tantamount to binding a monarch to the upholding of law, religion, and the protection of his people. In this view, the coronation ceremony is of great importance.

In France during the time of Joan of Arc, being crowned King wasn't quite so easy for the dauphin. By tradition, the coronation of French Kings was held at the

Cathedral of Reims, which had a long history of anointing the nation's ruling figures. The Merovingian King, Clovis I, a key personality in the founding of France, was baptized in Reims in 498-499 with holy oil. This gave the site some gravitas when it came to the anointing of its country's rulers, though it took a while before it became the traditional coronation site of French kings in the 11th century. Eventually, between the years 1027 to 1825, no less than 29 French Kings would be crowned at Reims.

Charles VII was almost not among them.

He was the son of the King, but he was not the eldest. His older brother died in 1417 when he was 14 years old, making him the heir to the throne. He lived in the same tumultuous time as Joan of Arc, and as the dauphin of a contested kingdom, he was especially in danger. When his side lost their country's capital in 1418, he had to flee south. It was also the year he took on the role of regent for his deranged father, Charles VI. When his father died in October, 1422, he became the de facto King of France. He inherited staggering problems – financial shortages, failed reconciliation attempts with the Burgundians, and the English and its French allies gaining ground. His enemies held the north – including Reims. He was reportedly feeling discouraged, and was perhaps considering giving in to the pressure exerted by the English forces and having a quiet life of retirement away from it all. But around this time, a peasant girl with a message came knocking – rather insistently – at his door. She believed she would be able to help her country, and her dauphin. She

was going to get him crowned at the
Cathedral in Reims.

Breaking the Siege of Orléans

Henry V of England passed away in
1422, before the mad Charles VI of France
whom he was supposed to be the successor
to under the Treaty of Troyes. Charles VI
passed away just a few months later the
same year. Henry V and Catherine's son,
Henry VI of England, therefore became the
King of the "double monarchy," not his
legendary father who had been behind
England's military victories over the French
and who had secured the treaty of 1420.
Little Henry VI who was nine months old at
the time, had northern France including
Paris. But down south with the
'Dauphinists,' the Armagnacs were still

championing the claim of the late French King Charles VI's eldest son, the crown prince, Charles of Valois.

With Henry VI still so young, his uncle, John the Duke of Bedford, took on the duties of a regent. His goal was to strengthen the English positions in the north, and then make a push southwards. Key to this southern offensive was the strategic city of Orléans, which maintained a loyalty with the Dauphin, Charles VII. The English began its siege on October, 1428. It was in many ways, the beginning of the end for the English claims in France.

In early 1429, Joan of Arc was received at court by the dauphin Charles, and she was able to correctly identify him from a sea of faces. To further her credentials, she also gave him a sign of God, something that only the King would be able to identify. She might have echoed a prayer the dauphin had made to God. Whatever this sign was, for it remains unknown, it was enough for Charles to take her seriously, even if he was unable to trust her immediately or completely. He foisted her off to some churchmen and theologians hailing from Chinon and the University of Poitiers for weeks of questioning and examination. Eventually, these trusted experts concluded that Joan had authenticity, chastity, humility and piety. It was enough of an endorsement for Charles to allow her into his service armed with considerable assets.

Joan of Arc was made the titular leader of a force that included veteran commanders leading an estimated 10,000 to 12,000 men. In accordance with her objectives, they were to head to Orléans and break the months' long English siege there. She was an inexperienced 17-year-old girl in the company of seasoned warriors, but she reportedly soon displayed an insight for battles and a commanding attitude beyond her years and gender that would win many a man over. In some ways, her severe limitations gave her mission more cachet and gravitas, for where else would "the Maid" acquire her talents, other than the divine voices that have long guided her?

Furthermore, while it may seem unfathomable now – why would anyone give an untried, minor female an army? - there are understandable reasons why, in Medieval Europe, someone like Joan of Arc would have been able to command as much resources as she had for her divine mission.

Medieval Teenage Warriors. First, her tender age might not have been as much of a deterrent to military service as it might seem at first glance. Information on the average age of soldiers at the time period is limited; there are not enough conclusive written documentation, nor are there enough representative excavations of medieval remains. But what is known is that whether or not young people comprised a significant percentage of the fighting forces of Medieval Europe, there is no question that they did exist on the fields of battle at around the time.

"The Children's Crusade" – a popular religious movement that swept across Europe in the 13th century comprised of youth. It was short-lived; un-sanctioned by religious authorities; so unsuccessful not one of them is believed to have achieved his goals of reaching and fighting for his faith in the Holy Land; and its legacy as a "youth movement" debatable. But young people were conspicuously part of the "Crusaders," and this has repeatedly been seen in surviving records from around the time period. In the Hundred Years' War itself, one of its most iconic of its figures, England's "Black Prince" Edward, began his legend on the Battle of Crecy at the age of 16. He held a position of great danger in the vanguard. His father the King, said the prince should have the opportunity to "*win his spurs*." It was a battle won by the English.

The Power of Religion. Thus Joan of Arc's tender age, while probably more the exception rather than the rule in medieval soldiers, still did not prevent her from participating in the fight. Her leadership position, however, was anomalous. Edward "The Black Prince" was required by his status as the English King's son to have military prominence as well as an image of courage and prowess - and he was educated accordingly. Joan of Arc did not have that background. Here then, we see the power of her religious credentials. And at the time, the religious argument for leadership could be a very compelling one; wars and its outcomes were heavily imbued with spirituality, sometimes considered as suggestive of divine judgment. In this light, her titular leadership of an army seems a fair proposition for a religious visionary able to prove her authenticity; she was not the first, nor was she the last. Joan of Arc was just especially distinctive because she managed to live up to her titular leadership at a crucial point of the Hundred Years' War.

The Changing Role of Women.
Medieval Europe was undoubtedly a patriarchal society with defined roles for men and women. As a matter of fact, underlying the Hundred Years' War was a gendered issue – can the throne of France be inherited by a female or through the female line? The precursor of the war after all, was the death of Charles IV, who had no sons but infant daughters. French authorities skipped the girls and crowned a cousin traced from the male line, Philip VI. Also skipped over was the English King Edward III, who would have had a closer claim through his mother. The answer therefore was a hard "No" on the question of female heirs, which

says a lot about the lesser position of women in society at the time.

This is aligned with the popular idea that women were relegated to domestic and/or subservient and/or peripheral roles in the medieval world. But they were very much an influential part of society wielding considerable power and authority, from the most distant fields to the centers of power. This is due to a multitude of factors.

A hundred years of war meant that men-at-arms, whether they were lords and leaders or masses of soldiers, have had to leave many of the affairs at home in the hands of women as they went off to battlefields. These included manual, financial and administrative types of work. Women could be found toiling in professions long-associated with men, including the forging of armor and weapons. Sometimes absences were temporary; in other instances as created by war – capture, injury, illness, death – the absences were more permanent and women had to adjust accordingly. Aside from war, illness also played a factor in the increased role of women. Some diseases, like the Black Death, reportedly claimed more men and children than they did women. Furthermore, at a time of Kings and Princes, indisposed leaders who were underage, at war or injured or ill or perhaps mad (as more than a few monarchs ended up being, including spells for Charles VI) - meant increased roles for their wives and mothers (sometimes, also their influential mistresses). This is on top of the usual roles that women of the upper echelons of society have played in terms of brokering alliances through matchmaking and marriage; the careful management of their royal children; strengthening relationships and improving the image of their men through "soft power;" and interceding with the sovereign on behalf of various causes. Sometimes, women were even sent into the fields of battle in titular roles comparable to what had been given to Joan – as religious visionaries, or symbolic aristocrats representing their fathers, husbands or sons. Other times, they really did go into the thick of things. Jeanne De Montfort, Duchess of Brittany, (1310-1376) repelled French attacks upon her husband's hotly contested estate after he was captured and imprisoned. Another noblewoman of the time period, this time from Scotland, Agnes Dunbar (1312-1369), became a legend for her defense of her husband's fortress against the English under Edward III. The French also had a heroine, in

Julienne du Guesclin (1333-1405), an Abbess. There was even a powerful female figure in the court of the dauphin, Charles of Valois; his mother-in-law, Yolande of Aragorn, was relied upon for her strategic mind, gift for deal-making, and her finances. She was an early champion for Joan of Arc, recognizing quickly that the young religious visionary could be instrumental to their cause.

This is how a teenage, uneducated, inexperienced girl found herself in a position to make real changes in the theater of a long-running war. Her youth and gender were uncommon but not unheard of, and her spirituality made a compelling argument for the times. Perhaps it was also a contributing factor that the dauphin was war-weary, described as indecisive and lethargic, and running out of options anyway. Her temperament almost certainly played a part too. She was said to be very charismatic and acted with authority, and indeed she gathered inspired believers and followers even before her legend-making turn at Orléans.

It also helped that along the course of her campaign, she displayed unexpectedly impressive, some say divinely inspired, talents for warfare that would increase her participation on the fields beyond being just a figurehead. Her courage and determination eventually commanded the attention of veteran warriors and captured the imagination of countless men, successfully inspiring even those previously unwilling to support Charles VII in the fight against the Anglo-Burgundian alliance.

A Stopover at Blois and Checy. Before heading to Orléans, she is said to have made a stopover at the town of Blois, which was close to the fighting. According to scholars, she met her army there and she first focused on repairs to the spiritual life at camp. There was the typical mix of drinking, prostitution, love affairs, gambling and swearing that seemed to trail most of the world's fighting forces no matter the place or time period. But Joan of Arc would have none of it. She reportedly required the marriage of unwed lovers, the departure of mistresses, and regular Mass and confession among the troops. She prohibited looting of civilians, and even put a stop to swearing. It should have been a tall order for an eclectic army which included nobles, veteran soldiers and mercenaries, but many followed.

She was described as being generally quiet and sweet, with a preference for keeping to herself – that is, until she perceived an offense against God that she would then address with what would later become a famous temper. She preferred being alone, but sometimes kept company with her aristocratic commanders, or a group of clergy. She was beautiful and shapely, even in the soldier's garb she donned to blend in; her men, however, would be quoted as saying she was somehow exempt from their desires. Others would even go so far as to say they found no compulsion to sin while in her presence. Still, part of her practice was to sleep in full armor, as if in protection of her chastity.

They set out from Blois and three days later, she met Jean, Lord Dunois, the 26-

year-old commander defending Orléans. Dunois was known as *"le Batard d'Orléans"* (it was no slander to his character or how he conducted himself in the siege, but a rather matter-of-fact reference to his lineage and the circumstances of his birth to the mistress of a nobleman). They met at Checy, across the river from where she wanted to be – which was, unsurprisingly for the passionate girl, right wherever the English were. Dunois met the full force of her personality because she disapproved of the move which had been done for her safety, especially given an unfavorable wind that was giving her army's barges difficulties at crossing. Her words included a rebuke on how God's counsel was *"safer and wiser"* than that of the men who had thought bringing her to Checy was a good idea. Witnesses would attest that her speech heralded a literal change in the wind, that would allow for a partial crossing of her army. The others would have to follow later.

Arrival at Orléans. Joan arrived at Orléans on the 29th of April, 1429. By this time, Orléans had already been under siege by the English for months, starting in October of the previous year. The English tactic was reportedly to attack with a small force that, while unable to mount a quick, conclusive siege, would be enough to starve out the garrison there. For a time it seemed to be working; there looked as if there was no easy way to break through the English's tightening noose. But then came that fateful day in April. Joan is said to have come under cover of night from the eastern gate of the city, while a French team distracted the opposing English on the western side. Her late arrival may have been due to concerns about the English, and/or to prevent her from being mobbed by the people eager to see her, having heard of their savior's impending arrival. She was met by adoring crowds nonetheless, pressing against each other for a touch of her person or even the white horse she had rode in on. By many accounts, she came in like an angel of God.

She was inspiring on her own, but had also arrived with much-needed reinforcements and supplies. This further boosted the morale of the French garrison in Orléans, as well as their chances of emerging victorious. Prior to her arrival they had been a demoralized group, with many carrying the recent loss at the Battle of Herrings just weeks prior, and now caught in a city that was being closed in by English forces on three sides.

Joan had her work cut out for her. The English had created a chain of fortresses using entirely new structures and modified existing ones (including churches), to close Orléans in. How is one to break such a well-entrenched siege?

Hard fighting did not start right away. The French side found it prudent to wait for the other men Joan had with her, who could not make the crossing at the same time she did. In the meantime, she sent out a series of messages to the English soldiers, asking them to leave. In one such message prior to battle, she reportedly stated, *"I am sent here in God's name, the King of Heaven, to drive you body for body out of all France..."* These were not taken seriously, and were often responded to insultingly by the bilingual English officers, some of whom used their knowledge in colorful taunts against her decency, and even derided her background by calling her "*vachere*" – a girl who looks after cows. This early on, she was also being called a sorceress. In spite of this, Joan was even willing to state her message in person at several points, asking the English to surrender in God's name. But only rejections and insults followed. The English were clearly not going to budge, at least not under the request of "*La Pucelle*" - the "Maid" sent by God. They were going to have to settle things on the field of battle.

While waiting for the rest of her men, Joan busied herself with church, familiarized herself with the English fortifications around Orléans, and made herself visible to the townspeople hungry for her presence. She even took escorted tours about the streets.

But the quiet would only last so long. The rest of the reinforcements arrived – a bit thinner than it originally was according to some reports, with losses of men attributed to desertions in Joan's absence. The English had supplies and reinforcements coming in too. Joan of Arc was going to see battle, and soon.

A Late... But Timely Arrival. Joan's first experience of the fight for Orléans was in a battle she was actually late for. On the 4th of May, she woke suddenly, compelled by her guiding voices to go to battle against the English. What she did not know however, was that while she slept, soldiers had already engaged in combat around the fortified church of of St. Loup (one of the structures near Orléans that the English had modified for their ends). She was not duly informed by her commanders, or perhaps the page boy who had been assigned the task was remiss in his duties. Either way, she rushed into her armor and upon her horse, gathered her banner, and charged to where the fighting was.

The road to St. Loup gave the compassionate teenager a brutal preview of the horrors of war. There were grievous injuries upon her countrymen, and the sightless eyes of the dead. She ached and grieved for them. When she arrived at St. Loup she found the French struggling, but they wouldn't be for very long. The very sight of her spirited charge renewed French efforts, and soon, the English defenses all but collapsed. Reinforcements would also be rebuffed soundly, leaving St. Loup in the hands of France. They had chipped at the

English's months' long siege and everyone knew it.

Joan made a gracious victor. She advocated for mercy upon Englishmen who were dressed (either genuinely or in disguise) as clergymen and captured along the course of battle. She grieved and wept for her dead enemies. She also encouraged her victorious side to make their confessions and give thanks to God. She was gracious and merciful... but she was also confident about one thing – the siege of Orléans, she said, would be broken in five days.

Five Days. Joan of Arc suspended fighting on holy days, which meant that of her prediction / prophecy / promise that the English siege would lift in all of five days, they all actually had less time to work with than that. On the 5th of May, the Feast of the

Ascension, there was no fighting but she did send an arrow flying toward the English – it came with a letter that her enemies derided as coming from a whore.

The opposing side was not the only one dismissive of her, however. She was to many still either a child or mad or only a woman or all of these things, certainly inexperienced and perhaps even an interloper, an unproven titular commander. Even those who did not subscribe to these beliefs were perhaps just unsure of her place in the command structure or what precisely they could expect from her and what they ought to do with her. Either way, when it came to deciding plans and strategies before and during the next days of fighting, the doors and decisions were barred to "*La Pucelle*" and even upon telling her of the plans, she would not even be privy to the entirety of it. This was displeasing to the "Maid," but she had her own "counsel-" that which she had with her God, which she was sure would prevail.

She was right, and along the course of her campaign, not even injury would seriously derail her from being an inspiration to the army. Fighting resumed on the 6th of May, with the French gaining ground toward the most critical fortress held by the English in the area – Les Tourelles. When the day's fighting ended, they had already captured the strongholds headed toward it - the fortified church of St. Jean-Le-Blanc and the fortified monastery of the Augustins. This was thanks in no small part to a daring rally led by Joan of Arc and one of her most loyal commanders, Etienne

Vignolles who was better known as "La Hire" for his own hot temper (he would also be known for her positive moral influence on a man who, before he fought by her side in most of her campaigns, had been known for boisterousness and vulgar language).

Next on the agenda was Les Tourelles itself. During fighting on the 7th of May, she was struck by an arrow between the neck and shoulder, an injury that she reportedly expected and foretold. It was painful and fairly serious, but she barely missed a beat. A quick dressing and she was back in the thick of things, and her determination was so inspiring the English eventually gave in.

By the 8th of May, the English were retreating and, being a Sunday, the pious Joan decided against pursuit. They had taken back Orléans, according to Joan's divine schedule.

Interestingly, the 8th of May was also a major feast day for St. Michael the Archangel.

The Battle Standard of Joan of Arc.

Of the accounts above, it is interesting to note that they mention Joan of Arc's rallying presence in battle, but do not speak of her actually fighting. Indeed, literature about Joan do not speak of her actually killing anyone. She was certainly there in her armor, and she would be remembered most prominently in that raiment; she also inspired men to raise their swords and she certainly had her own… But this was a war heroine who did not personally fight or kill her enemies. Off the field she tried to seek diplomatic solutions first and in their rejection, try to contribute to strategies. But on the fields she functioned more like an impulse-driven mascot, her banner almost always in her hands.

Joan's banner is said to have measured 3 feet by 12 feet. It was long and white, made of a material that resembled canvas and lined by a fringe of silk. The banner was adorned with the image of God holding the world while flanked by two angels, and had the words "Jhesus Maria" written upon it. Joan of Arc used the banner, which she claimed to love more than her sword, to point the direction of a rally. The white banner would have been a prominent sight in the chaos of a battle. She used two other flag-like implements in her campaign. A triangular pennon featuring the Virgin Mary, the archangel Gabriel and the French kingdom's symbol of a lily was held by a squire and used to show where she was in a battlefield. She also had a banner depicting the Crucifixion, around which men gathered for religious activities in accordance with her exhortations for the army to be more pious and in keeping with her own devout practices.

A Promise Kept at Reims

The victory at Orléans got everyone's attention, but the French court under the dauphin, Charles, was not quite ready – and indeed, never would be - to completely trust in Joan of Arc's judgement or prowess, nor yield their fates to her messages. She actually had to urge Charles into Reims for his own coronation. She was eventually successful in convincing him and his advisers, and Joan of Arc and her followers took Charles through hostile territory, engaging only as needed, until they reached Reims in 1429. By some accounts, the road there was a "bloodless" one - a miracle in itself if it is accurate that by her name alone were the English-occupied towns along the way subdued.

True to Joan of Arc's stated purpose, Charles VII, King of France, was crowned in Reims like many a French king that came before him. She was prominently at his side, beloved banner in her hands.

The Heretic

At this point of her life, Joan of Arc had shown her prowess at breaking the siege in Orléans and in enabling her dauphin to be crowned as Charles VII at the Cathedral in Reims. She had become quite beloved amongst her people, and was very much appreciated by her King, Charles VII. But it was the peak of her active contributions and achievements during the Hundred Years' War.

Certain factions of Charles VII's court was finding her too powerful. It also became rapidly clear that her approach and that of Charles VII was very different; he was cautious and more diplomatic. She on the other hand, just wanted to move forward with her mission. Her insistence on pressing the French efforts toward retaking Paris for example, ultimately proved unsuccessful and did not endear her to many. Her image is also said to have taken a dent for fighting held on a holy day, that of the Virgin Mary's birthday on September 8th, when she was also wounded in the thigh.

In 1430, not long after her legend-making victory over English forces at Orléans and delivering on her promise to Charles VII for his crowing at the Reims, she was captured by her enemies in a confrontation with the Burgundians at the town of Compiègne. She was paraded and displayed triumphantly by her foes and kept for months before she was eventually sold to the English for the king's ransom of some 10,000 livres.

A trial soon followed. If she was used to give Charles VII legitimacy, she was seen by their enemies as a way to discredit him. Among the accusations leveled against her were witchcraft and heresy. One of the basic ideas at the time was that if she was an authentic messenger of God, why would she experience failure and capture? Consequently, if she was not of God, then whose influence was she acting under? By implications like these, Joan of Arc then became more and more of a liability rather than an asset for the very King she had fought so hard to crown. Even if Charles VII fully believed in her divine mission (which was reportedly not the case), it had become politically disadvantageous for him to be associated with her so he distanced himself and apparently made no serious efforts at negotiating for her release or arranging for attempts to rescue her. In the cruel, dog-eat-dog, material world of kings and princes, it is often the innocents left to pay the ultimate price.

The common belief is that she was burned at the stake for being a witch. That was not exactly the case. She was tried in English-held Rouen by an ecclesiastical court for a laundry list of accusations. By most accounts she had held up well against her accusers; it was reportedly why her trial began as a public affair before it was closed off, why she may have been tortured; and why the 70 or so charges brought against her were eventually whittled down to her most prominent offenses, relating to wearing men's clothing and her claims of Godly communications.

In 1431, she was offered life in prison for a signed confession of her sins and a promise of reforming her behavior. She might have agreed out of fear of the punishment of execution by burning, and/or possibly because she was illiterate and did not completely understand what she was signing. Either way, she would defy it just a few days later. One of the reasons was that while kept in a military prison (as opposed to a church prison more befitting her situation), she felt threatened by her male guards while wearing female clothing. She was at risk of torture and rape, so she went back to her old ways of wearing men's clothes. She also claimed to hear her voices again, which were displeased with her decision to give in to her accusers.

These allowed her judges to convict her as a "relapsed" heretic, which led her to the stake at the marketplace of Rouen on the 30th of May, 1431. She requested for a cross to look upon as she died, and was mercifully accommodated. Thousands were said to have been present as she burned, including many who found themselves weeping and/or afraid, like the executioner who was reportedly worried at the idea of having burnt a saint. Legend has it that her heart survived the flames.

This is but one of many tales told of her death, the truth of which may be found somewhere in between fact and fiction. It was said that she died from smoke inhalation, but was burnt repeatedly because her organs survived. The third effort ended with her ashes scattered in the Seine.

For a long time, it was believed and hoped that some of these ashes were recovered from the foot of the pyre. Controversial relics found in a Paris apothecary in 1867 seemed to suggest this, and in the early 2000s, a team of international scientists were allowed to study them. The initial findings, shared publicly in 2006, seemed promising. The femur of a cat was revealed, which would have been in keeping with the medieval custom of tossing a black cat into the pyre of a witch. A piece of cloth recovered from the apothecary also seemed to fit in with the period. Hopes of finding answers were also raised by the existence of technology that could determine the age and regional origins of the cloth, the gender of the remains, the age of the deceased, and how many times the body was burnt over a limited period of time. These, according to researchers, would help differentiate and identify Joan of Arc from other people who may have been executed in a similar fashion. By 2007, however, the remains recovered in 1867 would be found falsely attributed to the saint. They appeared to be that of an Egyptian mummy, the powdered remains of which were used as medicine in olden days. The mummified bones were from around the 7th to the 3rd Century B.C., with the cat bone dating to the same time and also mummified. No DNA could be retrieved from the sample. Wherever the remains of Joan of Arc ended up, it was not in any known human hands.

After her death, the brutal war she had helped turn would go on for two more decades. But her short participation was like the proverbial tossed pebble that caused wide, rippling effects.

First, the English defeat at Orléans showed they were not invincible and that their victory was not inevitable. It may or may not have been a factor in decisions like that of Philip the Good, whose switching of sides would be a major blow to English ambitions. Philip the Good is said to have realized the English needed native collaborations to succeed in their goals for France and by 1435, he decided he was no longer willing to give it to them. He recognized Charles VII. By 1436, Paris was under the control of the French King. Other victories followed for France (especially with England embroiled in the Wars of the Roses, which were partly caused by their flailing efforts in France to begin with) until eventually, England had only Calais (which would later also be relinquished).

The French won and Charles VII kept his crown. He and other influential voices eventually fought for a retrial for Joan, and she was cleared by Pope Calilixtus III in the 1450s. She was declared a martyr. While this may seem like a way for Charles VII to right a wrong, it is believed that he was politically motivated to pursue Joan's innocence because, as her conviction discredited him, her acquittal served to lend the now victorious French King more legitimacy.

The Icon

Being declared a saint is the final step of a long, complicated process. There is waiting period to see if the person being considered has an enduring impact that can stand the test of time. Petitions are made at various levels of the Church, and the consequent collection and examination of documentation can take years. Votes are made as the case for sainthood goes up the ladder of approvals – and this is before and after the required number of miracles that must be attributed exclusively to the candidate saint, which should pass careful documentation and examination to determine if the miracle could not be explained by natural causes or other intercessors.

It's a long and complicated process and longer and more complicated for some saints than others. Joan of Arc had to wait until 500 years after her death, before she was canonized by the Roman Catholic Church in May 16, 1920.

Now, almost 100 years after that centuries' awaited canonization, she is still the subject of much conjecture. Depending on the belief systems one might subscribe to, there can be contentment with the belief that Joan of Arc was indeed a true messenger of God, that she had heard authentic saintly voices and these are the things that allowed her to do all the amazing things she was able to accomplish. Some saintly stories end thus. But by the sheer amount of documentation available on her life, telling of a story so compelling and a personality so strong, many people just could not help but delve into other possibilities.

The Ambitious Genius. From the individualistic lens, some consider the possibility that she was just an ambitious genius who used the idea of "voices" so that she may be listened to in a male-dominated, hierarchical society, with the motivation being she wanted to find a way to elevate her status. An opportunistic streak was not beyond her family, at any rate. For a time, her brothers are said to have reaped benefits of gifts and feasts while passing off an imposter as their sister for years after she was executed.

A Sick Girl. For those who prefer explanations from the medical field, theories abound as to the source of Joan of Arc's calling – she could have been hearing voices because she might have had schizophrenia (a disorder of multiple personalities), epilepsy, or any other disorder that causes hallucinations and delusions, including migraine, bipolar disorder, or brain injury. The "cowgirl," as she was derisively called by her English foes, may have even been suffering from bovine tuberculosis, contracted from unpasteurized milk and her exposure to the livestock she tended. There was also something not-quite saintly about her volatile temper, and she was not afraid to get physical. Raising her sword against her war opponents she might not have been willing to do, but there are accounts of her raising her hand against people from her side if they did something she found offensive.

The Sexual Subversive. If one looked at her with a gendered lens, maybe she was subverting sexual norms by turning away from marriage, dressing like a man, participating actively at war and, as have been suggested in some corners, had relations with other women (she did wear men's clothes and spend a lot of time in the company of other girls at night, but her devotees say the clothes were worn for her to blend in with soldiers and for her to be taken more seriously, while the nighttime female companionship is a custom of the times for unmarried women to band together for warmth and safety, especially in camps overrun by men).

Propaganda Figure. From a political lens, some pundits say Joan of Arc as she was popularly known was more a construction than a real woman – an earnest religious visionary or a mad country girl perhaps, who bit off more than she could chew when she entered wartime politics and was shaped by the powers of the time into a legend they could use to their own advantage. When she outlived her usefulness, she was set aside.

In some ways this was true. Symbolism was – and still is – so important in politics. She became a beacon of hope, a rally for a flagging cause; why shouldn't any enterprising King use her for his own ends? Her image was groomed and outfitted, probably from the moment she was in the sphere of the politically adroit, Yolande of Aragorn. Just as she was outfitted for war with weapons and an army, her image was cultivated, and it worked for a time. She increased enlistments, motivated demoralized troops, spurred on exhausted soldiers on the field. She created fear and awe in her enemies. There is no doubting her sheer presence in the fields of battle, the mention of her name, the sight of her distinct banner… have won many a day for France. But just as she was celebrated in her victories, her legend diminished with a taste of loss, and so did the people who championed her. Even after her death, her canonization may have also been politically useful; at the time, the French were in war and hoping to rally her troops, and the Holy See was fighting the threat of communism and atheism, thus needing a symbolic religious champion in Joan.

How she was used, however, shouldn't automatically invalidate her good work or her claims of divine mission. They are mutually exclusive; she could have been an authentic visionary, and used by those around her (and after her) for their own ends at the same time. The only problem here is how to parcel fact from fiction. How much of the deeds attributed to her really happened? Are proofs of her prophesies all biased by hindsight? Are some of the tales about her embellished? There will be no conclusive answer to these, in spite of all the written documents available about her person. Even contemporary accounts were contrasting, which is not an uncommon occurrence given the chaos of war. What is known for sure and widely corroborated though, is certainly heroic (and perhaps even saintly) enough – she was a peasant girl who had managed to do a staggering amount of things even if she began from nothing. She boldly set forth to shape the world according to her vision of what was right. She preached piety and devotion to God and lived by example. She bled for her country. She burned for her beliefs.

The power of her image and iconography is such that long after her death, Joan of Arc continued to be used for political purposes. It was used to rally Frenchmen in the Franco-Prussian wars of 1870-1871. Her image has been used by anti-Semites, nationalists and far-right political figures in the 1900s. She was a powerful symbol for the Allied forces in World Wars I and II, vilifying the Germans (especially when their bombs damaged the Cathedral at Reims). In France, her image resonated because of German aggression in the areas where she grew up; for the Americans and the British, her image was used to encourage women to participate in the effort by buying bonds. Over the years of her afterlife, her image proved so powerful and malleable that it found propagandist appeal to almost anyone. Those championing the monarchy, but also those who believe in self-determination, meritocracy and a republic; all spectrums from the right to the left; in every war or conflict the French found themselves; for women, for the LGBTQ community.

For all its good and bad, she has grown beyond her original objectives. It is almost talismanic (though she would likely not wish it to be so given her devout nature), how her image is conjured time and time again, for a miscellany of reasons. One can only hope that the powerful, enduring image of this pious woman will only be used wisely, with the same mercy and compassion she had even for enemies, toward a better world.

Printed in Great Britain
by Amazon